Eighty Per[cent]
of Success is
Showing Up

Over 100 Famous People Share
Their Insights into Life and Living

Edited by Les Krantz

BARNES
&NOBLE
BOOKS
NEW YORK

1993 Barnes & Noble Books

ISBN 1-56619-500-4

Imagine a room filled with the greatest achievers of the century. The spectrum is as broad as Billy Graham to Sophia Loren, Joe Louis to Jonas Salk, Lucille Ball to Bernard Baruch. If they've reached the pinnacle, they are there, awaiting your questions about what catapulted them to the top.

Based on what they have said before when asked to reflect on their towering success, the common denominator of their responses is its succinctness and simplicity. Unlike most people, they don't believe that success is based on a complicated formula of behavior; rather they attribute it to one or two things they believed in or did. The simple premises that they accepted, others rejected. The simple things they chose to do, others chose not to do.

As you read their statements, stop and think before you turn the page. Is there an application in your life, perhaps even one that does not immediately meet the eye? There are probably many of them. It is entirely possible that one or more of the pages that follow will help something wonderful happen in your life.

Les Krantz

*Eighty percent of success
is showing up.*

Woody Allen
Film Maker

If you think you can, you can.
And if you think you can't,
you're right.

Mary Kay Ash
Chairman, Mary Kay Cosmetics

*What the caterpillar calls
a tragedy, the Master
calls a butterfly.*

Richard Bach
Novelist

I think knowing what you cannot do is more important than knowing what you can do.

Lucille Ball
Entertainer

Don't try to be a jack-of-all-investments. Stick to the field you know best. Don't buy too many different securities . . . have only a few which can be watched.

Bernard Baruch
Financier

*If you can't write your idea
on the back of my calling card,
you don't have a clear idea.*

David Belasco
Playwright

*If you want
a thing done well,
do it yourself.*

Napoleon Bonaparte
Emperor

Don't think! Thinking is the enemy of creativity. It's self-conscious, and anything self-conscious is lousy. You can't try to do things; you must do them.

Ray Bradbury
Novelist/Screenwriter

Don't try to be one of the boys. Be yourself. Capitalize on your female strengths and use the psychological tools you have acquired to deal with male chauvinism as well as to climb the ladder of success.

Dr. Joyce Brothers
Psychologist

I get satisfaction of three kinds. One is creating something, one is being paid for it, and one is the feeling that I haven't just been sitting on my ass all afternoon.

William F. Buckley, Jr.
Editor/Writer

*When you reach for the stars,
you may not quite get one,
but you won't come up with a
handful of mud either.*

Leo Burnett
Founder, Leo Burnett
Advertising Agency

*I've always believed that
life is a lot easier if you're able to
laugh at yourself. And it's a lot
more fun, too. Whenever I do get
serious it does not last too long,
because I'm always thinking of
a humorous finish.*

George Burns
Actor/Comedian

To the discouraged, the doubting, or the despairing, what I had been presuming to say in films: Friend, you are a divine mingle-mangle of guts and stardust. So hang in there! If doors opened for me, they can open for anyone.

Frank Capra
Motion Picture Producer/Director

*It takes 20 years to make
an overnight success.*

Eddie Cantor
Entertainer

Three-quarters of the people you will ever meet are hungering and thirsting for sympathy. Give it to them, and they will love you.

Dale Carnegie
Author, *How To Win Friends And Influence People*

I don't think necessity is the mother of invention—invention arises directly from idleness, possibly also from laziness—to save oneself trouble.

Agatha Christie
Novelist

The price one pays for success is the inevitability of failure. I strongly believe though that the person who has never made a mistake is the person who has never accomplished much.

Joan Collins
Actress

The superior man thinks always of virtue; the common man thinks of comfort.

Confucius
Philosopher

*I don't know the key to success,
but the key to failure is trying
to please everybody.*

Bill Cosby
Actor/Humorist

The human body experiences a powerful gravitational pull in the direction of hope.

Norman Cousins
Editor/Author

Interdependence is a higher value than independence.

Steven R. Covey
Author, *The Seven Habits Of Highly Effective People*

The person who wants to make it has to sweat. There are no short cuts. And you've got to have the guts to be hated.

Bette Davis
Actress

*First and foremost, there can
be no prestige without
mystery, for familiarity
breeds contempt. All religions
have their tabernacles, and
no man is a hero to his valet.*

Charles de Gaulle
Former President, France

Give yourself a pat on the back, a pat on the back, a pat on the back.

Kirk Douglas
Actor

*A man's accomplishments in
life are the cumulative
effect of his attention to detail.*

John Foster Dulles
American Statesman

Be nice to people on your way up because you'll need them on your way down.

Jimmy Durante
Entertainer

A man is a success if he gets up in the morning and gets to bed at night and in between he does what he wants to do.

Bob Dylan
Singer/Songwriter

My old drama coach used to say, "Don't just do something, stand there." Gary Cooper wasn't afraid to do nothing.

Clint Eastwood
Actor

The reason a lot of people do not recognize opportunity is because it usually goes around wearing overalls looking like hard work.

Thomas Edison
Inventor

The gift of fantasy has meant more to me than my talent for absorbing positive knowledge.

Albert Einstein
Physicist

A platoon leader doesn't get his platoon to go by getting up and shouting and saying ,"I am smarter. I am the leader." He gets men to go along with him because they want to do it for him and they believe in him.

Dwight D. Eisenhower
34th President of the U.S.

It's them that take advantage that get advantage in this world.

George Eliot
Novelist

Nothing great was ever achieved without enthusiasm.

Ralph Waldo Emerson
Poet/Philosopher

*Ride the horse
in the direction
that it is going.*

Werner Erhard
Founder, est Training

Just don't give up trying to do what you really want to do. Where there is love and inspiration, I don't think you can go wrong.

Ella Fitzgerald
Singer

You have to be turned on by the thought of doing something well. It's doing something better than it has ever been done before, or creating a new refinement in what you're making or a better service than the other guy. This is how you build a business.

Malcolm Forbes
Publisher, *Forbes* magazine

Nothing is particularly hard, if you divide it into small jobs.

Henry Ford
Founder, Ford Motor
Corporation

*Men are strong only so long
as they represent a strong
idea. They become powerless
when they oppose it.*

Sigmund Freud
Physician

Don't accept that others know you better than you know yourself.

Dr. Sonya Friedman
Talk Show Host

. . . imagination is stronger than knowledge. . . dreams are more powerful than facts. . . hope always triumphs over experience.

Robert Fulghum
Author, *Everything I Need to Know, I Learned in Kindergarten*

Don't fight forces, use them.

Buckminster Fuller
Engineer/Architect

*In economics the majority
is always wrong.*

John Kenneth Galbraith
Economist

Find a void and fill it.

J. Paul Getty
Businessman

Courage is contagious. When a brave man takes a stand, the spines of others are often stiffened.

Billy Graham
Evangelist

Do your job and demand your compensation—but in that order.

Cary Grant
Actor

*All profoundly original work
looks ugly at first.*

Clement Greenberg
Art Critic

If you want to quit, that's a good time to quit. But if you are not a quitter, you begin to think fast.

Joyce C. Hall
Founder, Hallmark Cards

Never look down to test the ground before taking your next step. Only he who keeps his eye fixed on the far horizon will find the right road.

Dag Hammarskjold
Diplomat

A man will be loved as never before when he is able to give his woman the greatest pleasure he can give her—an orgasm. And when he can do this every time . . . her love will know no bounds.

Naura Hayden
Author, *How To Satisfy A Woman*

If you will it,
it is no dream.

Theodor Herzl
Statesman

There is no fright in a bang, only in the anticipation of it.

Alfred Hitchcock
Director/Producer

Lose as if you like it;
win as if you were used to it.

Tommy Hitchcock
Polo Player

What do you do when inspiration doesn't come: be careful not to spook, get too wound up, or force things into position. You must wait around until the idea comes.

John Huston
Motion Picture Producer/Director

Those who believe that they are in the right are generally those who achieve something.

Aldous Huxley
Novelist

If I had to sum up in one word what makes a good manager, I'd say decisiveness. You can use the fanciest computers to gather the numbers, but in the end you have to set a timetable and act.

Lee J. Iacocca
Chairman, Chrysler Corporation

In the takeover business
if you want a friend,
you buy a dog.

Carl Icahn
Businessman

*Attitude, not aptitude,
determines altitude.*

Jesse Jackson
Civil Rights Activist

It's all right letting yourself go, as long as you can get yourself back.

Mick Jagger
Rock 'n Roll Artist

Be a yardstick of quality.
Some people aren't
used to an environment where
excellence is expected.

Stephen Jobs
Co-founder, Apple Computer Corp.

What convinces is conviction. Believe in the argument you're advancing. If you don't, you're as good as dead. The other person will sense that something isn't there, and no chain of reasoning no matter how logical or elegant or brilliant, will win your case for you.

Lyndon B. Johnson
36th President of the U.S.

Everyone has a talent. What is rare is the courage to follow the talent to the dark place where it leads.

Erica Jong
Author, *Fear of Flying*

Man needs difficulties; they are necessary for health.

Carl Jung
Psychiatrist

Some luck lies in not getting what you thought you wanted, but getting what you have, which, once you have got it, you may be smart enough to see is what you would have wanted had you known.

Garrison Keillor
Radio Host/Author

Whenever you're sitting across from some important person, always picture him sitting there in his underwear. That's the way I always operated in business.

Joseph Kennedy
Financier/Diplomat

*Only those who dare
to fail greatly can
ever achieve greatly.*

Robert Kennedy
Former Attorney General of the U.S.

*Birds sing after a storm,
why shouldn't we?*

Rose Kennedy
Presidential Mother

*Your confidence in a product
or venture must be strong. If
your feelings are lukewarm, you
need more information before
deciding the extent of your
involvement . . . the lesson is
simple; you can't sell anything that
you wouldn't buy yourself.*

Victor Kiam
Chairman, Remington Corporation

The ultimate measure of a man is not where he stands in moments of comfort and convenience, but where he stands at times of challenge and controversy.

Martin Luther King, Jr.
Preacher/Civil Rights Activist

Intelligence is not all that important in the exercise of power, in fact, it is usually useless.

Henry Kissinger
Statesman

One of the first rules of playing the power game is that all bad news must be accepted calmly, as if one already knew and didn't much care.

Michael Korda
Author/Editor

Frustration is your worst enemy. You have to continue to stop yourself from letting it drive you to make irrational decisions — or rely on your advisers to stop you. When we put a deal together, I have the ability to focus on exactly what we're working on and close everything else out.

Henry R. Kravis
Investment Banker

If you're worried about that last at bat, you're going to be miserable, you're only going to get depressed, but if you put a picture in your mind that you're going to get a base hit off him the next time, now how do you feel? I try to put positive pictures into the minds of my players.

Tommy Lasorda
Manager, Los Angeles Dodgers

Life is what happens when you are making other plans.

John Lennon
Singer/Songwriter

One can get as much exultation in losing oneself in a little thing as a big thing. It is nice to think how one can be recklessly lost in a daisy.

Anne Morrow Lindbergh
Poet

If you aren't fired with enthusiasm,
you'll be fired with enthusiasm.

Vince Lombardi
Football Coach

*A woman's dress should be
like a barbed-wire fence:
serving its purpose without
obstructing the view.*

Sophia Loren
Actress

Always remember the other guy's got to make a buck too. If you don't leave him a profitable option, you'll hit his hot button. I'm surprised how many people think you can throw a hand grenade at a competitor and expect he'll stand there and enjoy it.

Frank Lorenzo
Businessman

*Every man's got to figure
to get beat sometime.*

Joe Louis
Prize Fighter

*The best sex education for kids
is when Daddy pats Mommy
on the fanny when he comes
home from work.*

Dr. William Masters
Sex Researcher

*To be successful, a woman
has to be much better
at her job than a man.*

Golda Meir
Israeli Prime Minister

The world is an oyster, but you don't crack it open on a mattress.

Arthur Miller
Playwright

No man is great enough or wise enough for any of us to surrender our destiny to. The only way in which anyone can lead us is to restore to us the belief in our own guidance.

Henry Miller
Novelist

As you enter positions of trust and power, dream a little before you think.

Toni Morrison
Novelist

You can't build a strong corporation with a lot of committees and a board that has to be consulted at every turn. You have to be able to make decisions on your own.

Rupert Murdoch
Businessman

*Int... increasingly
val... information
soc... ecause there
...data.*

...itt
...uthor

Always, always—never talk about what you're going to do, and don't tell them what you're not going to do.

Richard Nixon
37th President of the U.S.

Whatever you do, you should want to be the best at it. Every time you approach a task, you should be aiming to do the best job that's ever been done at it and not stop until you've done it. Anyone who does that will be successful—and rich.

David Ogilvy
Advertising Executive

The secret of business is to know something that nobody else knows.

Aristotle Onassis
Businessman

I sweat. If anything comes easy to me, I mistrust it.

Lilli Palmer
Actress

The way I see it, if you want the rainbow, you gotta put up with the rain.

Dolly Parton
Singer/Actress

To follow, without halt, one aim: there's the secret of success.

Anna Pavola
Ballerina

Capitalize upon criticism. It's one of the hardest things in the world to accept criticism, especially when it's not presented in a constructive way. Turn it to your advantage.

J.C. Penney
Merchant

*Getting people to like you
is the other side of liking them.*

Norman Vincent Peale
Evangelist/Author

Test fast, fail fast, adjust fast.

Tom Peters
Author, *In Pursuit of Excellence*

Keep things informal. Talking is the natural way to do business. Writing is great for keeping records and putting down details, but talk generates ideas. Great things come from our luncheon meetings which consist of a sandwich, a cup of coffee, and a good idea or two. No Martinis.

T. Boone Pickens
Businessman

When I was a child, I entertained myself with daydreaming. I think that's where the imagination gets most of its exercise and its nurture, when you're a child . . . I still do that a lot. Because that's where my work comes from.

Sidney Poitier
Actor

Great men can't be ruled.

Ayn Rand
Novelist/Philosopher

*Stand up. Look 'em
in the eye and tell
'em what you know.*

Dan Rather
Anchorman, CBS Evening News

The absolute truth is the thing that makes people laugh.

Carl Reiner
Writer/Producer

Courage is doing what you are afraid to do. There can be no courage unless you're scared.

Eddie Rickenbacker
Aviator

We are very short on people who know how to do anything. So please don't set out to make money. Set out to make something and hope you get rich in the process.

Andy Rooney
Journalist

*You always pass failure
on the way to success.*

Mickey Rooney
Entertainer

Nine tenths of wisdom consists in being wise in time.

Teddy Roosevelt
26th President of the U.S.

Of course, there is no formula for success, except perhaps an unconditional acceptance of life and what it brings.

Arthur Rubinstein
Pianist

Anything you are good at contributes to happiness.

Bertrand Russell
Philosopher

Courage is based on confidence, not daring, and confidence is based on experience.

Dr. Jonas Salk
Physician/Drug Researcher

Competition is easier to accept if you realize it is not an act of aggression or abrasion . . . I've worked with my friends in competition. Whatever you want in life, other people are going to want, too. Believe in yourself enough to accept the idea that you have an equal right to it.

Diane Sawyer
Anchorwoman, ABC World News

When you can't solve a problem, manage it.

Robert Schuller
TV Evangelist

Just remember, once you're over the hill, you begin to pick up speed.

Charles Schultz
Cartoonist

Keeping a little ahead of the conditions is one of the secrets of business; the trailer seldom goes far.

Charles M. Schwab
Former Chairman,
Bethlehem Steel

*Reading is a means of thinking
with another person's mind;
it forces you to stretch.*

Charles Scribner, Jr.
Publisher

True love comes quietly, without banners or flashing lights. If you hear bells, get your ears checked.

Eric Segal
Novelist

I will have eternity to rest.

Andres Segovia
Guitarist

*You may be disappointed
if you fail, but you are
doomed if you don't try.*

Beverly Sills
Opera Singer

Forget your opponents.
Always play against par.

Sam Snead
Professional Golfer

Talent is always conscious of its own abundance, and does not object to sharing.

Aleksandr Solzhenitsyn
Author

In automobile terms, the child supplies the power, but the parents have to do the steering.

Dr. Benjamin Spock
Physician/Author

*The first problem for all of us,
men and women, is not to
learn, but to unlearn.*

Gloria Steinem
Former Editor, *Ms.*magazine

Beware of the big play;
the 80-yard drive is better
than the 80-yard pass.

Fran Tarkenton
Former-Minnesota Viking Quarterback

I think I had a flair for [politics] but natural feelings are never enough. You've got to marry those natural feelings with really hard work—but the hard work comes more easily when you are doing things that you want to do.

Margaret Thatcher
Former Prime Minister,
Great Britain

*All you need in life is
ignorance and confidence,
and then success is sure.*

Mark Twain
Novelist

Trust your gut.

Barbara Walters
Journalist

Just keep going. Everybody gets better if they keep at it.

Ted Williams
Former Boston Red Sox

Never buy a saddle until you have met the horse.

Mort Zuckerman
Publisher, *U.S. News*
U.S. News and World Report